www.finishinglinepress.com

A Casting Off

poems by

Annette Sisson

Finishing Line Press
Georgetown, Kentucky

A Casting Off

ACKNOWLEDGMENTS

I would like to thank the following literary journals for publishing poems in
this collection:

Zone 3:   "Solar Eclipse"
Rockvale Review: "What Rope Is For"

Publisher: Leah Maines
Editor: Christen Kincaid
Cover Art: Maggie Monteverde
Author Photo: Evan Davis
Cover Design: Leah Huete

Printed in the USA on acid-free paper.
Order online: www.finishinglinepress.com
             also available on amazon.com

Author inquiries and mail orders:
Finishing Line Press
P. O. Box 1626
Georgetown, Kentucky 40324
U. S. A.

Table of Contents

Spain, a Casting Off..1

Fog..3

Lake Hamilton, July 2017 4

Magnolia...5

A Life's Telling...6

Solar Eclipse 7

What Rope Is For...9

The Amphibious Body 10

Her Cosmos..12

First Day of March 13

Ode to Billy Collins...14

No Wisp of Fur 16

Birds and Trees, My Mother's Paintings 18

In memory of my mother,
Mary Esther,
who maintained an active creative life, come what may.
And with deep gratitude and love
to my husband,
Jimmy,
who is my first reader and steadfast encourager—
and to my daughter,
Evan Marie,
who shares my love of poetry and the arts.

Spain, a Casting Off
—for Evie

A few months ahead,
a few thousand miles away,
Madrid: city of white buildings,
alabaster castings of faces and bodies
glistening, commanding the plazas.

You will cast off for Spain,
cast your lot with a new family—
temporary substitutes.
Hermanos, madre, papa.
With just enough Spanish to be known,
you will find yourself both familiar and strange.

But aside from statuary, pediments, domes—

cast: a group of performers
cast: an aspect, downcast
cast: a shade of color
cast: a hard cover to protect a broken bone
cast: to heave a net or fling a line.

Your casting has nothing to do
with architecture, or fishing,
or broken bones,
though something does feel mildly shattered.
This casting of yours to España,
thrilling and needful, is to me
a shedding, an ache.

My mother's cancer, terminal
your brother's move to Florida
my career on the wane, unregarded
a marriage plodding on
friendships scattered and thin.

And you, half-circling the globe,
a slow tectonic shift,
a dull rumble in the heart.
Imminent. A casting off.

> And I am left on a kitchen stool
> at 2 a.m.,
> summoned to branches budding
> in a remote forest,
> etudes with byzantine fingerings
> I've never learned,
> exotic words I don't recognize.

And then,

to another casting off.
Another finding.
A summons from a place
much further away,
more acutely beyond
my knowing, more strange
and yet always more familiar
than the gleaming white
castings of Spain.

Fog

How the grey-white high rise
   diffuses into grey-white sky,
      the metal bones melding into cloud,
as if the hard lines quietly thinned
   as the steel expanded into vapor.
      How my mother's body loosens its hold

on earth and daylight, language
   and sense. How her hands that rise
      and jab at assailants in the blank air
still reach for a tissue, placing the box
   back on the table's edge, tenderly,
      how they wipe the rim of the bucket

that contains the wretch of her dry
   heaves. How her wide eyes in the
      bones of her grey face fix themselves
on me as she says my name, her
   thin voice wailing "sorry, sorry,
      sorry." How can she know this lament

is my own? How can she reckon that
   her eldest daughter, the one she still
      remembers, would press her toward the
precipice, already pictures her rising
   into mist, seamless like girders, glass,
      and sky—grey-white bones vanishing in fog.

Lake Hamilton, July 2017
—for JTD

Before the speedboats came out
for their clamorous goodnight runs,
we had the lake to ourselves, led
by the current under a whitening moon.
We paddled our kayaks around the perimeter.
Side by side, we watched the sky,
a canopy of brownish grey tinged
with the faintest streak of peach.
An ordinary evening. No waterfowl,
no fish breaking, the surface as still
and dark as a window with the shade drawn.

We turned into the creek head,
noting how the gray above us
slid into purple. And then we looked
to the right, where the trees on the shore flashed
such brilliant orange I swore
the woods had caught fire. The flames lit
the branches, searing the leaves, rose
into violet, a suffusion of color—
an alchemy, from coral to amethyst.

At the end of the cove, a blue heron,
seemingly carved from rock, nabbed
its evening morsel and lifted into
the darkening thicket. We headed back
to the dock; the sky flushed pink, the blue-
black descended, and the moon struck gold.

Magnolia

The magnolia's thick, brown leaves
cover all—
grass, weeds, sunflowers, pansies—
stacking up
like dirty laundry in the front yard.
A nettling presence.
The ones not fallen, rusty
leather against
a bright blue sky, are soon
impervious to brooms,
stuck in rakes. Heedless of
our labors,
they half-bury the small
shoots we tend.

If its voluptuous blossoms
are spirit, incarnate
bodies of blooming breath, and the seeds
the life-force
of lung and heart, the pods are surely
the body, protective,
resilient, barbed. But the leaves,
neither body
nor blood nor breath, strangle our living,
piling on
the fact of death. The spectacle of
lustrous white
flowers, the size of a baby's christening
gown, is no
compensation; it cannot
atone. The seed
pods, hard and sharp, cut
bare feet,
blood as crimson as the kernels
stowed inside.

A Life's Telling

A darkening sky cloudless
No sunset trailing away
A silver curve
almost imperceptible
poised high in this expanse
as blue as wild delphinium

A sliver beckoning
Not quite a comma
nor apostrophe
A perfect paren
but only one
The other vanished
unsure of where to enter
when to insinuate itself

Never a complete thought
Never luminous

A parenthetical remark
craving its wandering comrade
Part of a larger compounded sentence
that cradles the dawn
and parses every last inch
of the wide whispering dusk

Solar Eclipse

Now that their daughter is
buried, the grandsons huddled
in smaller coffins,
nearby, the parents pore
over the newspaper article,
horrified at how
easily each sentence
tells what they failed to
see coming.
              The mother
remembers warning her
five-year-old not to look
into the solar eclipse,
the febrile kiss of a world
unsettled. Swaddled in
nightfall, the girl obeyed,
petrified that she might
be blinded. That was
February of 1961.

Today Judy and her sons
are dead, finally killed
by a husband's silent
bullets. Her father
doesn't have to remind
himself that in all that
time he had never detected
a bruise. But he cannot
understand why the final
scene didn't sicken him.
How could it be that all
the bleeding was internal?

The mother sits at the table, her back bent forward, shading into newsprint. There are times when the quickening inside is so keen, the pierce can't be felt. When the moment subsides, she scribbles words on a page, hoping, hoping, that with the next solar eclipse, someone will feel compelled to look.

What Rope Is For

If she lived in this world,
no longer would she murmur
about her appetite for Wyoming—
rocks, feathers, an open hand,
a conjuring. Her desire
is flamingo, a train ticket
to Aberdeen, the shiny midnight
of Hollywood starlight on paper.
And Wyoming. What she has
is a campaign button, leftover
bread crusts, a length of rope
knotted in place, its other end
circling. If she clutches its swing,
perhaps abrading her unaccustomed
hands, then she might ride
the arc high, unfist her grip,
hurl herself into the tall
plains, ranging that wide
horizon, filling herself with the glint
of minerals, flash of kites,
the sated life of rock and feather.

The Amphibious Body
—for Lise

I.

Off the road a cow lowers herself
into ditchwater, relieving the day's weight
and heat. Her body shrinks as she curls
her legs. *Leviathan*, I think, and watch
the highway dissolve in a shimmer of dream-water. . . .

II.

Two summers ago we launched
pontoons on an Indiana reservoir,
its shores austere, withering
from a three-month drought.
Our group of thirty stared
Into the sky, sure the air would vaporize
the lake. But we dropped anchor
at midpoint. I dragged my hands
in the drab water, observing how
it cleared over my fingertips.

III.

              And what if
water lapped the vessel, alluringly,
or there was a stir in the air, nothing
like a zephyr, or the humidity dispersing—
simply the indolent atmosphere
being ventilated, somehow easing
itself? And what if we left the boat
to bathe in the lake, everyone willing
to join in, bob with floats,
pushing against the waves, yielding?
And then what if we glided together
as one, mermaids and mermen,

with tresses uncoiled, the water
arranging the plaits into graceful fans
wafting across an olive drape? What
if we looked below into the lake
to see that our bodies had blurred
into wavy lines, fingers fading,
arms and legs extending themselves,
incandescent, merging with
the others' nebulous parts?

IV.

What, what would it mean if we
remembered how as children
our bodies were the language of water?

V.

I dream my death as interminable
drowning. I watch the body
descend, long hair swirling
around the head. Nothing tugs
or pushes; gravity simply prevails.
The self dissipates, bones settle.
There is no mourning.

VI.

On land I am a creature
living among creatures.
I watch for ways to blur the lines,
remember the elegance of coalescence.
On land, I dream of water.

Her Cosmos

They built a cottage
from the forest's growth,
consecrated it
through rituals of morning,
routines of seasons, leaves
dropping, budding, greening—
sealed by the thick mud
of their life's steep slog.

Now at dark he lifts
her from chair to bed,
sees the last of her
tomorrows emerge from the trees,
the deer gathered, grazing
in the front yard, nipping
the tips of the fig trees.

And he knows
when they come again
from the undergrowth,
rising from their wild
nests, come to taste
whatever new has grown,
she too will rise,
carrying a loose bouquet
of cosmos like
those she planted
beside the porch, some
dropping silent on grass
as she, too, retreats
into mist and branches,
a veil of darkening shimmer.

First Day of March

February. An early spring of heavy
clouds. Torrents pouring, winds throbbing.
The storms drop their weight of rage, saltless
whips lashing the pane beside my face.
I melt into the frantic air. Slices
of fractured sky jackknife into earth.

Respite. And I am drawn into the mist
silvering out sky and land, a Monet,
the pale hues whitewashed, the river
now a half-mile expanse of lake
white capped, remnant chops of wind,
a towering pageant of eagle and gust.

First day of March. Still I watch
the sky and cannot feel what I know—
my mother's small pocket of earth, not
yet sheathed with turf, not yet
visited since that strangely bright
January day when we gathered.

The spring world this year, a muddy
tarp bucking wild against its tether.
Convulsions of shifting sky cover
sputtering fields, bodies rising and banks
yielding, trees wracked waist-deep
in roiling water. The sun still shade.

Ode to Billy Collins

Is not poetry a megaphone held up
to the whispering lips of death?
"Greece"

Your Greek question:
a meta-moment, a pause,
personifying the final
disintegration of things—
earned and unearned, people
and pillars, one and the same.
Death's silent blare
snuffs out our words,
our speaking, but not our
compulsion to leave towers
of stacked sand in our wake.
Ozymandiases all,
we are deaf, you
intone, to the thrum of our
voices uttering death's
speechless drone.

A surprising tack for you—
a reach for the invisible screen
between here and hereafter.

More often you take
the day's dregs and twist
them into oddly
pleasing stories straightly
told, using less
punctuation than I
thought possible, sparing
readers the weight of more.
An elegant lead, you
two-step me
lightly across the crowded

floor, tracing your own
startling patterns, then
jump on the train
snaking by, the sweaty
line undulating.
Provocative, prosaic.

But even as a poet
with a Grecian turn,
you are a familiar,
a household god
I heed. Your
swank, bold tenor
emanates from
the megaphone you
graciously hijacked
from death, giving me
back my lost words,
prodding me to hear
the faint murmur of my
own voice, my mouth
moving in the rhythm
of time, out of time,
like a poem, an echo,
like a classic present.

No Wisp of Fur

I haven't figured out where the dead go.
The owl in the quiet grass at the schoolyard's tree-lined edge;
The cat outside the sliding glass door,
        vanished with the TV's strobe of light;
The woods roaches murdered with impunity;
The doe, her body slowly plucked away
        by a coven of vultures;
The father, six inches lost to spinal compression,
        too small for his coffin;
The mother in her casket, gold crossed and red jacketed,
        roses splayed on a draped comforter
        of her own making;
The teenagers and children, their years spooled tightly;
The suicides, resigned; the snakes with no skins left
        to shed; the alligator father who eats
        his young; even the dead buzzard.

Perhaps they all gather in a splendor of spirit dance,
        turning and stepping, like
        the rise and fall of breath.
Perhaps they dance their way back to embodiment:
        an exhalation of pink dogwood,
        acres of rye grass fluorescent in early green,
        a cricket, its tegmen ecstatic.
Or maybe the steps bollix them.
They return, but rueful, clumsy.

Earth is no purgatory, no heaven.

Still the rhythm of their movements, lilting, shadowed,
        endues the twittering half-
        light of our waking.

Where have they gone?

Their bodies, sprinkled or oozing, merge with soil,
      the molecules breaking into atoms,
      earthworm, grass, tree. Residue.

What of the glistening thread of their lives,
      the halting heave of their leaving?

Toward something.

Death's mystery is nothing I can see, not even
      the faintest trace. Not even a nudge or hint, not even
      the prospect of something. Not even a barred owl
      in quiet grass. No wisp of fur in its curved beak.

Birds and Trees, My Mother's Paintings

I have scanned the tree tops
    to and from Indiana,
seeking out hawks.
    Miles of bare branches,
splinter into shards,
    then feather softly.

A dozen hawks perch high.
    One lands, a sweep
of dark accordion fans
    snapping closed beside a wide
cream belly. Muscular.
    Sturdy. Two test the smallest
limb with their heft, the sag and bend
    visible from the streak of road.

My mother's paintings of trees are birdless.

She gave me four oils
    of trees, one of a bird,
a scarlet tanager, but none
    of both together.

I want to ask her why.

She planted trees, kept
    the feeders full of seeds,
the birdbath brimming,
    the hummingbird stand sweet
with sugar water. She reveled
    when the phoebes reclaimed
their nest in the front porch
    rafters to brood again.

I have waited too long.

Fixed in her recliner, she
    can no longer explain
what I just thought to ask.
    Maybe she struggled with
proportions: birds to trees.

I still search for trees
    with hawks, robust and alive,
wondering if the phoebes
    will return this spring,
though she will be past knowing.

In the birds, the trees, the way
    she feathered oil on canvas,
I will remember the phoebes,
    the parents flying off for insects,
the chicks' mouths gaping.

Unable to escape Indiana until her 30th birthday, **Annette Sisson** has discovered, 30 years hence, that she misses the Hoosier state even though Nashville, TN, is a lovely place to have landed. For three decades, she has taught English at Belmont University, where her area of expertise is Victorian literature. Her life's calling and deep gladness have been to teach and mentor students. In her spare time, she plays the piano, bakes, supports the theater community, travels, teaches abroad, studies the birds at her feeders, reads, and writes. After raising three children with her husband, Jimmy Davis, and performing various administrative and leadership duties at Belmont, she knows how fortunate she is now to have time to devote to writing poetry.

CPSIA information can be obtained
at www.ICGtesting.com
Printed in the USA
BVHW031133050619
550226BV00001B/197/P